A Note to Parents

DK READERS is a compelling program for beginning readers, designed in conjunction with leading literacy experts, including Dr. Linda Gambrell, Professor of Education at Clemson University. Dr. Gambrell has served as President of the National Reading Conference, the College Reading Association, and the International Reading Association.

Beautiful illustrations and superb full-color photographs combine with engaging, easy-to-read stories to offer a fresh approach to each subject in the series. Each DK READER is guaranteed to capture a child's interest while developing his or her reading skills, general knowledge, and love of reading.

The five levels of DK READERS are aimed at different reading abilities, enabling you to choose the books that are exactly right for your child:

Pre-level 1: Learning to read
Level 1: Beginning to read
Level 2: Beginning to read alone
Level 3: Reading alone
Level 4: Proficient readers

The "normal" age at which a child begins to read can be anywhere from three to eight years old. Adult participation through the lower levels is very helpful for providing encouragement, discussing storylines, and sounding out unfamiliar words.

No matter which level you select, you can be sure that you are helping your child learn to read, then read to learn!

LONDON, NEW YORK, MUNICH,
MELBOURNE, AND DELHI

U.S. Editor Nancy Ellwood
Assistant Editor Liza Kaplan
Managing Art Editor Michelle Baxter

Designer Marc J. Cohen

Reading Consultant
Linda Gambrell, Ph.D.

First Edition, 2010
10 11 12 13 14 10 9 8 7 6 5 4 3 2 1
Published in the United States by DK Publishing
375 Hudson Street, New York, New York 10014

Created and produced by
Parachute Publishing, L.L.C.
322 Eighth Avenue
New York, New York 10001

DK books are available at special discounts when purchased in bulk
for sales promotions, premiums, fund-raising, or educational use.
For details, contact:
DK Publishing Special Markets
375 Hudson Street
New York, New York 10014
SpecialSales@dk.com

A catalog record for this book is available
from the Library of Congress.

ISBN: 978-0-7566-4452-9 (Paperback)
ISBN: 978-0-7566-4451-2 (Hardcover)

Printed in China
First printing January 2010

The publisher would like to thank the following for their kind
permission to reproduce their photographs:

ABBREVIATIONS KEY:
t-top, b-bottom, r-right, l-left, c-center, a-above, f-far,
bkgd-background

Front cover Catalinus/Dreamstime.com (br)
4 John Carnemolla/Shutterstock.com
5 Mike Brake/Shutterstock.com
6-7 Nancy Gill/Shutterstock.com (6);
vita khorzhevska/Shutterstock.com (7)
8 Elena Elisseeva/Shutterstock.com (t);
Sally Wallis/Shutterstock.com (b)
11 Condor 36/ Shutterstock.com (tr)

12-13 BESTWEB/Shutterstock.com (12c);
Michael Stokes/Shutterstock.com (13)
14-15 Michael Metheny/Shutterstock.com
(14); WhiteShadePhotos/Shutterstock.com (15)
17 Ulrich Mueller/Shutterstock.com
18-19 Tap10/Shutterstock.com (19)
21 Mahantesh C Morabad/Shutterstock.com (b)
22-23 Nancy Gill/Shutterstock.com (bkgd);
Robert Ranson/Shutterstock.com (22tl)
24-25 2265524729/Shutterstock.com (24);
Darrell Blake Courtney/Shutterstock.com (25t);
Wendy M. Simmons/Shutterstock.com (25b)
26 Stefanie Mohr Photography/Shutterstock.com (bkgd)
Bartlomiej Nowak/Shutterstock.com (tr);
28-29 Kirsanov/Shutterstock.com (28);
Deniz Ünlüsü/Shutterstock.com (29t); ason/Shutterstock.com (29b)
30-31 Rebecca Photography/Shutterstock.com (30);
DUSAN ZINDAR/Shutterstock.com (31)
32 Mahantesh C Morabad/Shutterstock.com (ft);
ason/Shutterstock.com (ct); Freaksmg/Dreamstime.com (c);
Robert Ranson/Shutterstock.com (b)

All other images © Deere & Company.
Every effort has been made to trace the copyright holders of
photographs, and we apologize if any omissions have been made.

Discover more at
www.dk.com

DK READERS

BEGINNING TO READ

1

JOHN DEERE

Good Morning, Farm!

Written by Catherine Nichols

DK Publishing

PARACHUTE PRESS

Cock-a-doodle-do!
The rooster is crowing.
It is morning on the farm.

Many chores need to be done
before breakfast.
Let's get going!

Cows live in the barn.
It is time to milk them.

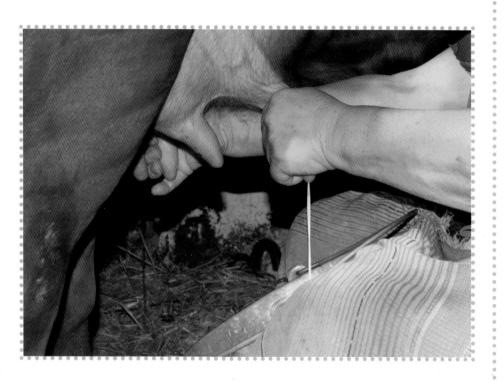

Squirt, squirt, squirt.

The milk goes into a pail.

The farm animals are hungry.
What do they eat?

Horses and sheep eat hay.

Cows eat hay, too.

The tractor makes sure
there is plenty of hay
for the animals.
It brings hay to the barn.

Horses go to the pasture.

The pasture is full of green grass.

Horses eat grass as well as hay.

A fence keeps the
animals safe inside
the pasture.

pasture

Who lives in the hen house?

Chickens do!

Every morning their eggs
are collected.

The pigs are getting a new home.
The Gator brings wood for a pen.

The new pen is just the right
size for the pigs.

The Gator is stored in a shed.

Other machines are
kept there, too.

The shed protects the machines
from bad weather.

Wheat grows in the field.

When the plants are tall,
a combine harvests them
and turns them
into grain.

grain

The grain is stored in the silo. One day the grain will be used to make bread.

silo

What is growing in the garden?
Beets, lettuce, peas, and other
good things to eat.

Animals like to nibble on the vegetables.

A scarecrow watches over the garden.

orchard

Apple trees grow in an orchard.
The trees are planted in rows.

Tractors made for orchards
are just the right size to drive
through the rows.

Honeybees make sweet honey.
They live in hives.

hive

Is the honey ready?
Yes, it is.

The chores are done.
It is time to go inside
for breakfast.

Look at the good food to eat.
It comes from the farm.
Yummy!

Glossary

Grain
The seeds of grasses such as corn, wheat, rye, oats, and barley

Hive
A box where honeybees live and make honey

Orchard
A group of fruit or nut trees, usually planted in rows

Pasture
Land where grass is grown for animals to eat

Silo
A tall building or tower where grain is stored